BIG SPORTS BRANDS

# ADIDAS
## Athletic Apparel Trailblazer

by J. R. Kinley

SportsZone

An Imprint of Abdo Publishing
abdobooks.com

abdobooks.com

Published by Abdo Publishing, a division of ABDO, PO Box 398166, Minneapolis, Minnesota 55439. Copyright © 2024 by Abdo Consulting Group, Inc. International copyrights reserved in all countries. No part of this book may be reproduced in any form without written permission from the publisher. SportsZone™ is a trademark and logo of Abdo Publishing.

Printed in the United States of America, North Mankato, Minnesota.
052023
092023

Cover Photo: Matthew Ashton/AMA/Corbis Sport/Getty Images
Interior Photos: Daniele Badolato/Juventus FC/Getty Images, 4–5; Nattawit Khomsanit/Shutterstock Images, 7; Christof Stache/AFP/Getty Images, 8; Brauner/Ullstein Bild/Getty Images, 10–11; Bettmann/Getty Images, 12, 15; Ullstein Bild Dtl./Ullstein Bild/Getty Images, 13; S. Vannini/De Agostini/Getty Images, 17; Werner OTTO/Ullstein Bild/Getty Images, 18–19; AFP/Getty Images, 20; Alexandre Loureiro/Getty Images Sport/Getty Images, 21; Neil Baylis/Alamy, 23; Michael Ochs Archives/Getty Images, 25; Getty Images Publicity/Getty Images, 26; Julian Finney/Getty Images Sport/Getty Images, 28–29; Gary M. Prior/Getty Images Sport/Getty Images, 30; Juan Manuel Serrano Arce/Getty Images, 31; Adam Bettcher/Stringer/Getty Images Entertainment/Getty Images, 33; Catherine Steenkeste/NBAE/Getty Images, 34–35; Gotham/GC Images/Getty Images, 36; Alexander Hassenstein/Getty Images Sport/Getty Images, 38; Gilbert Flores/Variety/Getty Images, 39; Bebeto Matthews/AP Images, 40

Editors: Steph Giedd and Priscilla An
Series Designer: Joshua Olson

**Library of Congress Control Number: 2022948903**

**Publisher's Cataloging-in-Publication Data**

Names: Kinley, J. R., author.
Title: Adidas: athletic apparel trailblazer / by J. R. Kinley
Other title: athletic apparel trailblazer
Description: Minneapolis, Minnesota: Abdo Publishing Company, 2024 | Series: Big sports brands | Includes online resources and index.
Identifiers: ISBN 9781098290658 (lib. bdg.) | ISBN 9781098276836 (ebook)
Subjects: LCSH: Adidas USA (Firm)--Juvenile literature. | Sports--Equipment and supplies --Juvenile literature. | Brand name products--Juvenile literature. | Sports clothing industry--Juvenile literature.
Classification: DDC 658.827--dc23

# TABLE OF CONTENTS

*Chapter One*
## THEY OWN SOCCER ...................... 4

*Chapter Two*
## SMALL START, BIG IDEA ............ 10

*Chapter Three*
## NOT JUST SHOES: ADIDAS EXPANDS ....................... 18

*Chapter Four*
## BIG BRAND, BIG NAMES ............ 28

*Chapter Five*
## THE BRAND PEOPLE KNOW ....... 34

TIMELINE  42
IMPORTANT PEOPLE  44
GLOSSARY  46
MORE INFORMATION  47
ONLINE RESOURCES  47
INDEX  48
ABOUT THE AUTHOR  48

*Chapter One*

# THEY OWN SOCCER

Kameron has started soccer practice. He is on a club team now, and he wants to be good. Last year's shoes are too tight, however, so his older sister Sienna is taking him to buy new cleats for the season. She plays for her high school team. He has always worn his older sister's hand-me-down shoes. But this year he can finally get his own.

Rows of colorful soccer cleats greet them when they enter the sporting goods store. Kameron is overwhelmed by his options. He picks up the first shoe he sees.

Paul Pogba is one of Adidas's elite players.

> ### It's in the Name
>
> Adidas is popular not only in the United States. It is a major brand in countries across the world. In the United States, people pronounce the name "Uh-DEE-dus." But in European countries, such as Germany and the United Kingdom, people say it differently. They pronounce it "AH-dee-das." The pronunciation comes from the founder's name: Adi Dassler.

"What about this one?" he asks Sienna, holding up a blue pair of shoes.

"Hmmm. Let's look for Adidas shoes," Sienna says. "They own soccer."

Kameron nods. He knows what she means. Many famous players and coaches wear Adidas. His eyes skim through rows of cleats until he spots a red-and-gold shoe with the iconic three stripes.

A store employee comes up to them. "Would you like to try those on?" he asks Kameron. His name tag reads "Jorge."

"Sure," Kameron says eagerly.

"These are the Nemeziz. It's a good choice. I'll find you a pair in your size."

Jorge opens a box and hands Kameron a shoe. They smell fresh. He looks closely at the black laces and cut-out ankle before slipping his feet into the shoes.

"Lionel Messi used to wear this style. They were designed for speed and agility or quick changes in direction. That's what Messi is known for," Jorge notes.

The Adidas Nemeziz shoes are associated with soccer player Lionel Messi.

Kameron takes some steps in them. When he bends his feet, the shoes flex.

"We also have Adidas Speedportals," says Jorge. "That's what Messi wears now."

"I like the Nemeziz shoes." Kameron smiles. He jogs in place and imagines that he is dribbling a soccer ball on the field. He feels excited about the upcoming season. Wearing the Adidas cleats makes him feel as if he could score a couple of goals.

Kameron and Sienna walk to the checkout counter together. "Why do you think Adidas *owns* soccer?" Kameron asks his sister.

"I don't know. They just do."

Many Adidas shoes are known for their classic three-stripe design.

## How Does a Brand Rise to the Top?

There are many brands of athletic shoes. Adidas is one brand that stands out from the others. As with other famous makers, people want to buy its merchandise. Superstars ranging from Lionel Messi and Patrick Mahomes to Beyoncé wear Adidas gear.

The Adidas story began more than 100 years ago. The founder, Adi Dassler, wanted to make the best-quality athletic shoes. He began making shoes as a teenager. Dassler wanted athletes wearing his shoes to have the edge in competition.

Now, Adidas makes shoes, equipment, and clothes, but not just for sports. Its shoes and clothes are worn by people for everyday activities. Sports clothing and items such as hats and shoes are now part of everyday fashion. People like to wear them because of how they look. Adidas's history in sports helped it become a trailblazer for sports brands.

## Chapter Two

# SMALL START, BIG IDEA

Young Adolph (Adi) Dassler was born in a small town called Herzogenaurach in Bavaria, Germany. His mother oversaw a laundry business, and his father was a tailor in a shoe factory. At first, Adi trained as a baker, but he was more passionate about sports. Adi was extremely athletic and competed in various sports, including soccer, boxing, and track and field. While participating in these different sports disciplines, he noticed that the athletes all wore the same shoes. That gave him the idea of designing shoes that met the specific demands of each sport. He thought that personalized shoes

Adi Dassler was the iconic founder of Adidas.

Germany was on the losing side of World War I. After the war, the country had to give up land and reduce its military.

could give the athlete an advantage. But before he could make his idea a reality, World War I (1914–18) began. Since he was a German citizen, Adi was required to join the army.

Adi was just 19 years old when he returned home after World War I. Germany's economy was not doing well. People could not afford to buy new shoes. But since shoes were made of leather, people could keep them for many years. Adi made a living repairing shoes for people in his town. He used his mother's laundry shed as his workshop. But he also had big ideas beyond this small repair shop in Bavaria.

## Making Shoes

In 1924 Adi formed Dassler Brothers Sports Shoe Factory with his older brother Rudolph. With three workers, they made track shoes and soccer shoes. Their shoes had hand-forged metal spikes. This was new at the time. The spikes provided better grip on surfaces, which gave athletes more speed.

As the economy recovered, sporting events became very popular. The Dasslers' business grew, allowing them to hire more people. They also purchased machines to make large numbers of shoes faster. With the new people and equipment, the shoe factory relocated to a large brick building.

Adi wanted elite athletes to use his shoes. He thought this would prove their quality. The main sporting events he targeted were the Summer Olympics and the World Cup. But first Adi partnered with the

Having a factory made shoemaking go a lot faster.

German national track-and-field team. He wanted its athletes to use and test his shoes. With their feedback, Dassler and his company were able to improve the designs.

Dassler gave track shoes to German distance runner Lina Radke to wear in the 1928 Summer Olympics in Amsterdam. Radke was wearing Dassler shoes when she won the 800-meter race, setting a new world record.

In addition, the German Olympic track-and-field team was successful in 1932 and 1936. These successes boosted the Dassler shoes' reputation. However, there was another athlete at the 1936 Olympics in Berlin who brought Adidas even more attention. Jesse Owens, a US track-and-field star, wore Dassler shoes as he broke records and won four gold medals.

Sadly, not long after the Olympics in Berlin, the world was at war again. The Dassler brothers were not able to operate their shoe business. After the Allied forces defeated Germany in World War II (1939–45), the Dasslers were able to restart. But in 1948, Adi and Rudolph decided to split the company. Rudolph went on to form Puma. Adi registered the name Adidas in 1949,

> **Choosing the Name**
>
> Adi Dassler originally wanted to use the name Addas for his company. It was rejected because there was already a company registered with a similar name. So he added the *i* and called his company Adidas.

Jesse Owens broke many records in his career across track-and-field events, including sprinting, long jump, and hurdles events.

along with the trademark three stripes. He wanted his shoes to be recognized by the stripes for brand awareness. Adidas and Puma are still headquartered in the same small town of Herzogenaurach, Germany.

## Owning Soccer

The 1954 World Cup gave Adidas a chance to make its name in the soccer world. The Hungarian team was dubbed "unbeatable" that year. They had won the Olympics and dominated the world soccer stage. West Germany faced them in the final, which was in Bern, Switzerland, and won. The match became known as the "Miracle of Bern."

Traditional soccer "boots" were designed primarily to protect the foot. They were heavy and covered the ankles. This is what the Hungarians and the other teams wore. However, Adidas designed shoes for the West German team. Its shoes were much lighter, about half the weight. The shoes were cut out around the ankles, and the laces went farther down the toe. There was also extra padding. Screw-in studs on the bottoms of the shoes could be adjusted for different field conditions. When the West German team defeated the Hungarians to win the World Cup, Adidas suddenly gained worldwide fame.

As the years passed, Adidas continued to earn respect among soccer pros. In 1965 West German soccer player Uwe Seeler tore his Achilles tendon. This could have ended his career. But Adi Dassler designed a special shoe

### The Original

By the 1960s, Adidas had grown to be one of the largest sports-shoe companies in the world. Adi Dassler had become wealthy and successful, but he remained humble. He was most comfortable among athletes, working to make better products to improve their performance. Dassler died in 1978 at age 77.

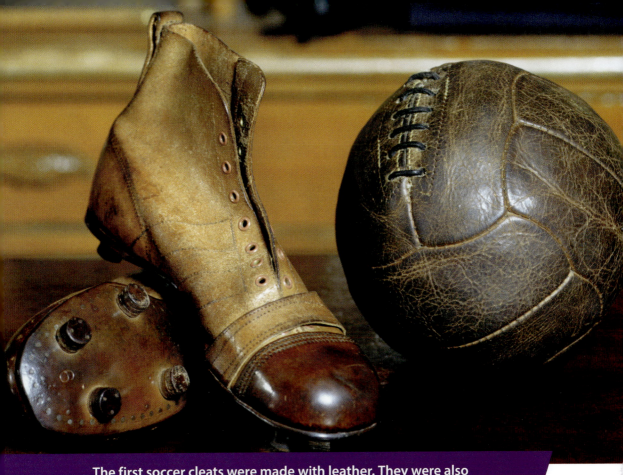

The first soccer cleats were made with leather. They were also very heavy.

for Seeler. The heel construction and cushion took pressure off the tendon and provided extra support. Seeler was able to continue playing soccer that season. He even helped West Germany reach the final of the 1966 World Cup. Other players with similar medical conditions were able to keep playing because of these orthopedic shoes.

*Chapter Three*

# NOT JUST SHOES: ADIDAS EXPANDS

Adidas continued to expand its business in the realm of sports. It has made new and improved professional athletic shoes, equipment, and clothing. The brand has delved into many sports, including soccer, football, basketball, baseball, wrestling, volleyball, swimming, and golf.

Athletes are not Adidas's only consumers. The brand has numerous products for everyday people who need athletic gear for school or for their hobbies. Whether it be running, hiking, or yoga, Adidas has the perfect products.

Although Adidas started out with a focus on selling athletic shoes, it expanded to include various products for its customers.

## Modernizing the Soccer Ball

Not only did Adidas modernize soccer shoes; it also modernized the soccer ball. Adidas designed the official ball for the 1970 World Cup in Mexico. At the time, soccer balls were made with 18 leather panels. There were no markings on them. The new ball was made with 32 panels, which were a mix of hexagons and pentagons. It made a more perfect sphere than old models. In the 1970s, many soccer fans watched games on black-and-white televisions. The panels on the ball were black and white, so viewers could see the ball better on TV. They named the ball Telstar, for being the star of television. The black-and-white-patterned soccer ball has become an icon for the sport. Since then, every official World Cup ball has been made by Adidas.

Adidas continues to innovate the Telstar design for each World Cup. The Tango design was introduced in 1978. Each hexagonal panel had a triangular pattern with

The introduction of the Telstar changed the way soccer balls were made.

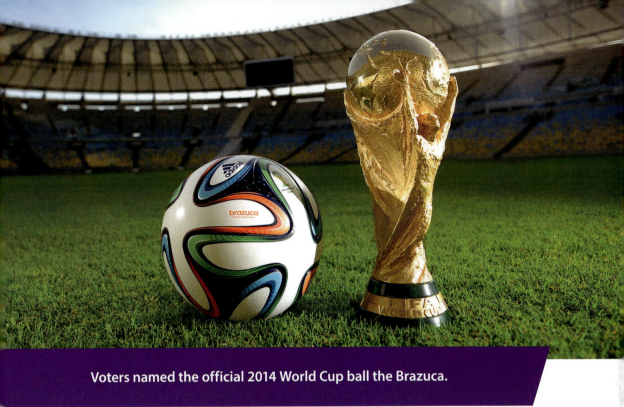

Voters named the official 2014 World Cup ball the Brazuca.

arches, and the arches formed larger circles. The design was popular and lasted for 20 years. In 1986 the World Cup ball was created with synthetic materials for the very first time. This improved performance in wet conditions. For the 1998 World Cup in France, Telstar had color. The Tricolore was red, white, and blue, the colors of the French flag. The Jabulani was used in South Africa in 2010 and was made of only eight panels. It was made to be more spherical. However, the difference in its smooth design proved problematic to players. The ball moved differently at various speeds than previous models. So, the Brazuca, designed for the 2014 World Cup, reverted to more seams, which resulted in more predictable flight paths.

Almost 50 years after the first Telstar, Adidas produced the Telstar 18. It was made from sustainable, recycled material. It contained a chip to interact with smartphone users. "Developing the Telstar 18 while staying true to the original model was a really exciting challenge for us," said Roland Rommler, Adidas's director of football hardware. "The new panel structure and inclusion of an NFC (near-field communication) chip has taken football innovation and design to a new level."

## Apparel

By the 1960s, athletes were putting more thought into what they were wearing. Adidas took notice and made its first signature tracksuit in 1967. A tracksuit is a jacket and matching pair of pants made of breathable material. Many of them have a stripe down each side. The Franz Beckenbauer tracksuit, named after a famous West German soccer star, began the company's journey into making athletic apparel. In the 1970s, martial arts icon Bruce Lee wore the look, bringing it more attention.

Tracksuits continued to grow in popularity over the following decades. Adidas also began to make clothing for actual competition. Romanian gymnast Nadia Comăneci wore Adidas gear during the 1976 Olympics, where she became the first gymnast to ever score a perfect 10 in any event.

Adidas tracksuits were advertised everywhere, including Great Britain, in the 1980s.

Performance apparel has expanded to include many items. Buyers can find shorts, pants, shirts, jerseys, jackets, hoodies, gloves, hats, and more. Even socks and underwear are designed to give a competitive edge, because the designers consider factors such as breathability and fit.

## Sneakers

Sneakers and athletic clothing have become popular to wear every day, not just on the field or the court. People like how they fit and how they look. Hip-hop music group Run-DMC recorded a hit song called "My Adidas" in 1986. The company partnered with the group to promote their shoes.

Certain brands and styles of sneakers are extremely popular, so they attract hype and fans. They sell out and are collected or resold. Sneaker fans and collectors are called sneakerheads. Trends are often set by videos and ads featuring popular celebrities. Social media platforms such as Instagram have helped sneakerheads know and follow

### The Slide

Adidas first made the Adilette slide for the West German national soccer team in 1970. They were worn as shower slides to avoid foot disease in locker rooms. The Adilette was released to the public in 1972. They are waterproof and designed with suction cups on the bottom to avoid slipping.

Members of Run-DMC were typically seen sporting Adidas tracksuits and shoes.

Tennis player Stan Smith is the face of one of Adidas's best-selling shoes.

what is out there. For example, the Sneaker News account has more than 10 million Instagram followers.

Whether they are being collected or worn, there are some top sellers that seem to never go out of style. The Superstar came out in the 1970s for basketball. The shoe was leather with impact protection and good traction on the court. The Stan Smith sneaker was named after an American tennis superstar in the 1970s. They are still top Adidas sellers.

The Samba is an indoor soccer shoe that became casual wear. These shoes are especially popular in Europe. The Ultraboost running shoe came out in 2015 with heel-to-toe comfort. Music artist Ye, known then as Kanye West, drove up their popularity by wearing a pair. After Ultraboost, the similar NMD came out. There are various NMD editions, including designs by another musician, Pharrell Williams.

### Stan the Man

Before they were called Stan Smith tennis shoes, they were named for French tennis star Robert Haillet. But Haillet retired in 1971. At the time, tennis was becoming more popular worldwide. Smith was at the top of the sport. In 1978 Adidas renamed the tennis shoe after him. They became one of the top-selling sneakers of all time by any brand.

*Chapter Four*

# BIG BRAND, BIG NAMES

In the world of sports, brand partnerships are highly sought after. Partnerships with athletes and teams can produce many benefits. These include an increase in sales, brand awareness, and reaching a loyal and passionate fan base. Adidas has established its influence through its numerous partnerships with professional teams, individual athletes, leagues, and events.

Adidas is heavily involved in soccer leagues and competitions. The World Cup has been Adidas's world stage for marketing since 1970. Adidas has been the supplier of the official ball for all World Cup matches.

> Adidas has been a longtime sponsor of Real Madrid, a professional soccer club in Spain. In 2022 the team won the European Champions League.

During matches, soccer fans can also spot the Adidas logo on many national team jerseys, shorts, and shoes.

Partnerships with the best soccer clubs such as Real Madrid, Arsenal, Bayern Munich, and Manchester United are important. They make Adidas an essential brand in the soccer world. Additionally, its endorsement deals with top soccer athletes have helped Adidas gain worldwide fame. Argentine Lionel Messi and retired English superstar David Beckham are elite athletes who have lifetime deals with Adidas.

Beckham started his professional career with Manchester United in 1995 and played through 2013. He is best known for his amazing bending free kicks. In 1996 he famously scored from the halfway line. Adidas chose Beckham to promote the Predator in

David Beckham's 2002 Adidas campaign introduced the famous Predator Mania boots.

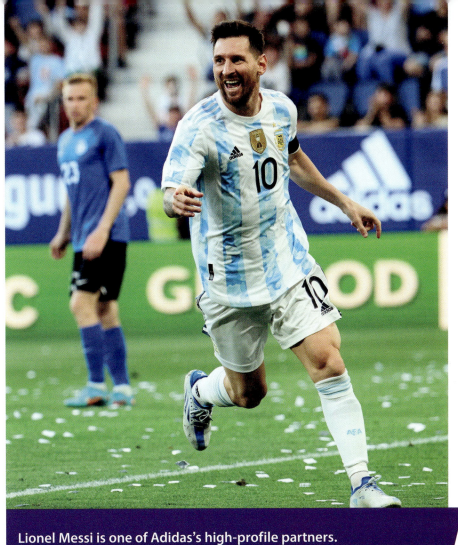

Lionel Messi is one of Adidas's high-profile partners.

the 1990s. The shoe was designed with rubber fins on the instep, which helped control kicks. They became very popular.

Messi is considered one of the greatest players in the history of the sport. The striker began thrilling fans with his amazing play as a 17-year-old for Spanish club Barcelona. Over the next two decades, his play for Barcelona, French club

Paris Saint-Germain, and the Argentine national team won him many honors. In 2021 Messi became the first player to win the Ballon d'Or Award seven times. That honor has been given to the best player in the world since 1956. Adidas has designed shoes with his name, and Messi wears different styles of Adidas when he competes, including the Adidas Nemeziz boots.

Adidas is not only a popular soccer brand. Its three stripes are proudly displayed in various sports leagues, including football, golf, basketball, swimming, baseball, and hockey. In 2021 the National Basketball Association (NBA) extended its partnership with Adidas. Adidas would continue to supply team-branded shoes, practice gear with the Adidas logo, uniforms, and other apparel.

The German sportswear brand also sponsors individual big-name stars such as Philadelphia 76ers guard James Harden, Portland Trailblazers guard Damian Lillard, and forward Candace Parker of the Chicago Sky. In football, Adidas sponsors quarterbacks Aaron Rodgers of the Green Bay Packers and Patrick Mahomes of the Kansas City Chiefs. Additionally, baseball's Kris Bryant, the 2016 National League Most Valuable Player, is sponsored by Adidas. Other professional sports partnerships include hockey superstar Sidney Crosby of the Pittsburgh Penguins and English golfer Justin Rose.

In 2022 Adidas began partnerships with US college athletes. The first group of athletes to sign endorsement agreements were 15 female student-athletes from different universities and sports. This included Erin Moss, a volleyball player for the Georgia Tech Yellow Jackets. Jameese Joseph, a soccer player from North Carolina State University, was another athlete who signed an endorsement deal with Adidas.

In addition to sponsoring physically athletic sports, Adidas is venturing into Esports. Esports are sports played via a video gaming system. In January 2021, G2 Esports, a European professional gaming organization, announced a partnership with Adidas. The two companies collaborated to produce an apparel line that included crewnecks, hoodies, and joggers.

Candace Parker has won two WNBA Championships and two Olympic gold medals. In 2022 Parker started a mentorship program with Adidas to help college athletes in their careers.

*Chapter Five*

# THE BRAND PEOPLE KNOW

Adidas is the largest sports brand in Europe and the second largest in the world. As of 2022, it was worth $36 billion. The strongest product sales for Adidas are in the Europe–Middle East–Africa (EMEA) region. In 2021 this region had 37 percent of total net sales, followed by North America at 24 percent. Sports shoes are still its top sellers, as about 53 percent of their sales are footwear. Apparel makes up 41 percent of sales, and equipment makes up the remaining 6 percent.

Derrick Rose has been an Adidas partner since 2011.

Celebrities such as Yara Shahidi sported clothing from Beyoncé's Ivy Park collection.

## Creative Big Names

Apart from sports partnerships, Adidas collaborates with well-known personalities. Celebrities are given more creative freedom for the products they create. This has helped Adidas gain customers of different backgrounds.

Music superstar Beyoncé was a creative partner with Adidas. In 2019 Adidas relaunched the singer's brand, Ivy Park. The collaborative collection featured apparel and footwear.

However, Beyoncé and Adidas parted ways in 2023 due to a significant drop in Ivy Park product sales.

Other celebrity brand partnerships include Humanrace, by musical artist Pharrell Williams. This collaboration features basic all-gender clothing, including hoodies, lounge pants, and sandals. Partnering with high-profile celebrities like Beyoncé and Pharrell Williams has helped Adidas connect customers with its products.

## Powerful Social Media Campaigns

Social media is another major medium that Adidas uses to interact with its broader audience. The brand has a large presence on social media platforms like YouTube, Twitter, TikTok, Instagram, Facebook, and Pinterest. This has allowed Adidas to use social media campaigns to stay relevant, bring in new customers, and increase its public image.

The 2022 campaign Run for the Oceans was a partnership with Parley for the Oceans, a nonprofit group that seeks to raise awareness for marine conservation and human-made pollution in the oceans. The organization also helps clean plastic waste. To participate in Run for the Oceans, people needed to download the Adidas Running App. Adidas pledged that every ten minutes of tracked running on the app would equal one plastic bottle cleaned up. This campaign not only

The German national soccer team participated in the Run for the Oceans charity run.

supported Adidas's commitment to sustainability. It also gave a chance for customers who care about the environment to interact with the brand.

Another way Adidas used social media to engage with its customers was during the 2020 Black Lives Matter movement after the murder of George Floyd. On its Instagram account, Adidas showed its support to the Black community. The brand made commitments to have an equitable hiring process. It also promised to increase representation within the company. Adidas set aside $120 million toward programs that were devoted to addressing racial disparity.

## Controversies

However, not all of Adidas's attempts at inclusion have been well received. In 2012 Adidas partnered with American fashion designer Jeremy Scott. They created the purple-and-orange JS Roundhouse Mid high-top sneakers with orange shackles, or ankle cuffs. Scott said he was inspired by *My Pet Monster*. This was a cartoon and toy from the 1980s that wore orange shackles. Before its release, Adidas advertised an image of the shoes on one of its social media accounts. The ad read, "Got a sneaker game so hot you lock your kicks to your ankles?"

The public's response to the new shoe was highly critical. People felt the shackles reminded them of slavery. American civil rights groups tried to stop the shoes from being released. Adidas responded, "[The shoe design was an] outrageous and unique take on fashion and has nothing to do with slavery. We apologize if people are offended by the design and we are withdrawing our plans to make them available in the marketplace."

**Jeremy Scott faced backlash after releasing a controversial shoe design.**

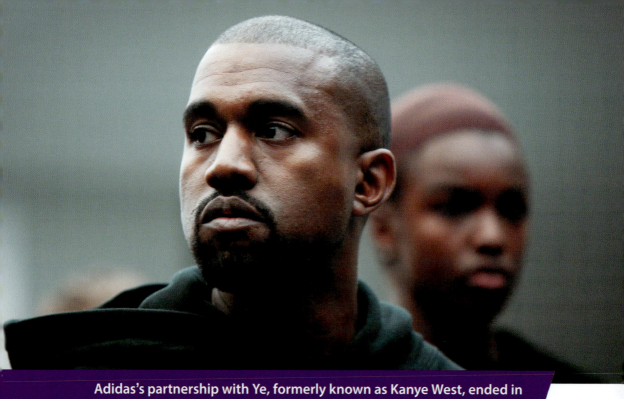

Adidas's partnership with Ye, formerly known as Kanye West, ended in October 2022 after his anti-Semitic comments on social media.

In 2022 Adidas ended their long-standing partnership with Kanye "Ye" West after the artist made a series of anti-Semitic comments on social media. Adidas had manufactured Ye's Yeezy brand since 2016, and their partnership was successful financially. The sportswear brand had said that their collaboration was "the most significant partnership ever created between a non-athlete and an athletic brand." Terminating the contract was likely to cost Adidas well over $200 million in 2022 alone. However, the public applauded the brand for its decision.

Adidas's list of controversies isn't just related to celebrities. In March 2020, the sportswear brand, along with other major brands, was linked to China's Uyghur labor camps. These camps in the Xinjiang region of China were revealed to be places where the Uyghur people were tortured and forced into labor. Public outcry and news spotlights led Adidas to promise that it would not source any material from the Xinjiang region.

## A Better Future

Although Adidas has made improvements in its mission toward sustainability, it still has a long way to go in terms of ethical labor. On the positive side, the brand has made a goal of having a system in place to identify and manage human rights issues. This includes making sure its supply chain workers have fair labor and safe working conditions.

"Own the Game" is one of Adidas's new strategies for the future. The sportswear brand plans to grow the brand across the globe in years to come. Its plan includes focusing on brand credibility, innovation, consumer experience, and sustainability. Adidas also hopes to invest in its employees, champion diversity, and expand its data and technology expertise. These strategies will ensure that Adidas will be a stronger and more credible company than before.

# TIMELINE

### 1924
Dassler Brothers Sports Shoe Factory is founded.

### 1948
The Dassler brothers split up their company.

### 1949
Adi Dassler registers "Adidas" and the three-stripe logo trademark.

### 1954
In the "Miracle of Bern," Adidas soccer shoes gain worldwide fame when the West German soccer team defeats the "unbeatable" Hungarians in the World Cup.

### 1967
Adidas produces its first tracksuit.

### 1970
Adidas produces the iconic Telstar for the World Cup.

**1986**

Run-DMC releases the hit song "My Adidas."

**1994**

The prolific Predator soccer cleat is released, made famous by soccer star David Beckham.

**2006**

Adidas signs Lionel Messi, one of the greatest soccer players of all time.

**2019**

Adidas begins a partnership with Beyoncé's brand, Ivy Park.

**2022**

Adidas ends its partnership with Kanye "Ye" West.

# IMPORTANT PEOPLE

### David Beckham
Former professional soccer player David Beckham first signed a sponsorship deal with Adidas in 1997. The company signed him to a lifetime contract in 2003.

### Beyoncé
Music artist and entrepreneur Beyoncé partnered with Adidas for her Ivy Park line.

### Adolph (Adi) Dassler
Adolph Dassler is the founder of Adidas.

### Lionel Messi
One of the greatest soccer players of all time, Messi first signed a sponsorship deal with Adidas in 2006. They signed a lifetime contract in 2017.

### Jesse Owens
Owens wore Dassler shoes when he won four gold medals in the 1936 Olympics in Berlin.

## Lina Radke

Radke was a gold-medal-winning track star on the German national team in the 1928 Olympics. She was one of the first athletes to promote Adidas.

## Jeremy Scott

This American fashion designer is known for his colorful and quirky designs. He has partnered with Adidas for apparel and shoes.

## Stan Smith

Born in 1946, Smith was an American tennis star when tennis and sneakers gained popularity. The Adidas sneaker named after him is one of the best-selling shoes of all time.

## Pharrell Williams

Williams is a music artist and entrepreneur who partnered with Adidas for his Humanrace line.

# GLOSSARY

**apparel**
Clothing.

**collaborate**
To work together.

**consumers**
Buyers.

**elite**
The highest level.

**icon**
A person or object well known for excellence.

**innovation**
A new idea about how something can be done.

**orthopedic**
Related to the bones and tendons.

**sustainable**
Causing little or no environmental damage.

**synthetic**
Manufactured, not natural.

**trademark**
A unique or distinctive feature or characteristic.

**trailblazer**
One who leads the way.

# MORE INFORMATION

## BOOKS

Dyer, Kristian R. *Innovations in Soccer*. Minneapolis, MN: Abdo Publishing, 2022.

Jenner, Caryn. *Sports Legends*. New York, NY: DK Publishing, 2019.

Nicks, Erin. *Lionel Messi*. Minneapolis, MN: Abdo Publishing, 2020.

## ONLINE RESOURCES

To learn more about Adidas, please visit **abdobooklinks.com** or scan this QR code. These links are routinely monitored and updated to provide the most current information available.

# INDEX

Beckenbauer, Franz, 22
Beckham, David, 30
Beyoncé, 9, 36–37
Bryant, Kris, 32

Comăneci, Nadia, 22
Crosby, Sidney, 32

Dassler, Adi, 6, 9, 10–16

Floyd, George, 38

Haillet, Robert, 27
Harden, James, 32

Joseph, Jameese, 33

Lee, Bruce, 22
Lillard, Damian, 32

Mahomes, Patrick, 9, 32
Messi, Lionel, 6–7, 9, 30–32
Moss, Erin, 33

Olympics, 13–14, 16, 22
Owens, Jesse, 14

Parker, Candace, 32

Radke, Lina, 14
Rodgers, Aaron, 32
Rommler, Roland, 22
Rose, Justin, 32
Run-DMC, 24

Scott, Jeremy, 39
Seeler, Uwe, 16–17
Smith, Stan, 27
Sneaker News, 27

West, Kanye "Ye", 27, 40
Williams, Pharrell, 27, 37
World Cup, 13, 15, 16–17, 20–21, 28
World War I, 12
World War II, 14

# ABOUT THE AUTHOR

J. R. Kinley is a writer and artist and has published titles depicting professional athletes. She is part of a sports family from Ohio. Her husband, Shaun Kinley, is a former NCAA wrestler at the Ohio State University and coaches a nationally ranked high school wrestling team. Together, they operate Kinley Studio.